THE
WOODBURNER
HANDBOOK

THE
WOODBURNER
HANDBOOK

A PRACTICAL GUIDE TO GETTING THE BEST FROM YOUR STOVE

ANTHONY BAILEY

First published 2015 by
Guild of Master Craftsman Publications Ltd
Castle Place, 166 High Street, Lewes,
East Sussex BN7 1XU

ISBN 978 1 78494 073 7

Publisher Jonathan Bailey
Production Manager Jim Bulley
Senior Project Editor Dominique Page
Editor Stephen Haynes
Managing Art Editor Gilda Pacitti
Designer Simon Goggin
Illustrator Alex Bailey

Set in Clan Pro
Colour origination by GMC Reprographics
Printed and bound in Turkey

CONTENTS

Introduction

MOST PEOPLE LOVE AN OPEN, CRACKLING LOG FIRE. It looks beautiful burning in the hearth and its flickering flames echo ancient times. In practice, however, an open fire is slow and inefficient, and its heat output can be disappointing. This is where that relatively modern contrivance, the woodburner, comes into its own. An efficient source of heat that comes to life quickly and can be contained without risk, it is a far cry from our ancient ancestors rubbing sticks to make a tiny spark from friction. This is 'the modern way of the flame'.

Anyone with the right sort of property and location can install a woodburner and enjoy both the practical benefits and the satisfaction that owning one brings.

It makes sense, then, that increasing numbers of people are opting for the independence and pleasure that ownership of a woodburning stove brings. The woodburner not only looks inviting, and provides a comforting heart and soul to the home, but its heat output can be fiercely impressive. Anyone with the right sort of property and location can install one and enjoy both the practical benefits and the satisfaction that owning one brings.

Right and above: A woodburning stove combines the best of both worlds – the warm, comforting glow of a log fire and the convenience and control provided by modern heating technology.

THE JOYS OF A WOODBURNER

The heart of a woodburner's appeal is that it fulfils
a basic need within us for a heat source that we can
entirely control, instead of being subject to the whims
of energy companies or a loss of supply due to bad
weather. But there are also plenty of other benefits
that make investing in one worthwhile.

Lower energy bills

Running costs for central heating are high, especially
in the winter months. With a woodburner you can save
a considerable amount by foraging for wood, and by
cutting and storing your own timber from all kinds of
sources. And if you follow the advice in this book, you
can ensure that your stove is always running at its most
efficient level, so you're not wasting money.

Versatility

A woodburner isn't just good for heating. Many a stove
can be found with a kettle steaming away on top. And
cooking on a woodburner is perfectly feasible. Even a
small one has room for a couple of saucepans on top,
and when it is running on a medium heat it is perfect
for cooking a casserole over a couple of hours. If you
choose a stove with a rear flue exit, then the whole of
the top is available for cooking. An alternative option
is to buy a woodburner with an integrated oven.

A slightly less decorous facility of a woodburner is its
ability to dry laundry. The heat is terrifically effective
at driving moisture from fabric, especially if the items
being dried are up near the ceiling where the heat
rises and circulates – a 'kitchen maid' clothes dryer
suspended from the ceiling is ideal for this. The safety
proviso is that nothing should be near enough to the
stove to present a fire risk, particularly if it consists of
man-made fibres or a lightweight fabric, which are more
vulnerable to heat.

Above: On grey, cold days there is nothing better than a woodburner for creating a warm, cosy atmosphere. It gives the home a focus and a beating heart. In contrast to central heating that seems soulless, a woodburner creates a comforting cushion of heat that spreads throughout the home.

Left: Some woodburning stoves incorporate a built-in oven. Even without this feature you can use the top of the stove for cooking. Many owners swear that it tastes better than a meal cooked on a gas stove or in an electric oven!

A 'greener' lifestyle

Any process of very rapid oxidation – or burning, as it is otherwise known – results in the release of carbon dioxide into the atmosphere. It is the build-up of this and other greenhouse gases that is responsible for climate change. So, is a woodburner really a more eco-friendly way to heat our homes? Most green campaigners believe that the release of 'ancient carbon' – such as coal, oil or gas derived from underground sources laid down as forests millions of years ago – is bad for the environment, and that this matter should be left buried underground. However, 'new carbon' – that is, growing woodland and forests – should be managed and cropped sensibly and sensitively, and the felled timber processed and used in the most efficient manner. This is because nature left unchecked runs rampant. Trees, bushes and undergrowth become an unruly mess that chokes itself. Burning wood as fuel therefore forms part of a natural cycle: it makes good use of felled or fallen trees, and makes space for new trees to be planted. Unlike fossil fuels or minerals, this supply of fuel is inexhaustible, so long as we look after our trees.

Above: Well-managed woodlands are a renewable resource – the timber that is cropped makes room for new trees to be planted.

Energy is not being supplied from hundreds or thousands of miles away, it is being created with your own bare hands.

A sense of satisfaction

When our woodburner is running I regularly go to the nearest log store, outside our back door, bring in a new sack of wood and empty it into the log basket. Then I go and get a bag of kindling and some newspapers. This all happens every day and sometimes more than once in an evening, depending on how inclement the weather outside happens to be.

Every week, that log store is refilled by wheelbarrow from one of the other stores at the bottom of our very long garden. This could all be seen as tedious. However, it's not such a chore if you think about the benefit you are getting from it. Energy is not being supplied from hundreds or thousands of miles away, it is being created with your own bare hands. For me, and for many others, this provides a profound sense of satisfaction that makes it well worth all the physical labour expended.

Above: Spending plenty of time outdoors gathering logs from your log store is a by-product of owning a woodburner..

A practical solution

I get to visit many woodwork shops and most, if not quite all, have either a woodburner or a heating system that uses wood-waste pellets or simply waste wood. It would be strange indeed if they didn't make use of their redundant wood material in this way.

Generally, for small workshops I recommend enclosed heating systems because there is no danger of dust igniting. Not everyone realizes that any dust, however inert, under certain conditions can be persuaded to explode – and this naturally includes flammable wood dust. However, it is important to make a distinction between 'lying dust' and 'flying dust'. A limited amount of dust and shavings lying around on the floor does not present a hazard, so a stove is suitable for this situation; just make sure flammable materials such as timber, varnishes, polishes and rags are kept well away from it.

Below: A woodburner is often the only practical solution for heating and cooking in a workshop, a caravan or on a narrowboat.

Canal boats, caravans and camper vans need heat for comfort and cooking, and a woodburner is often the only practical solution. There are, in fact, smaller stoves designed with narrowboats in mind. Essential safety measures include a sealed flue; a hardstanding for the stove, such as a concrete slab; and a carbon monoxide alarm.

Time spent outdoors

The woodburner appeals to our desire for a simpler, more down-to-earth lifestyle. It brings a natural element into even the busiest of working lives – something that commonplace 'flick-of-the-switch' central heating never can. If you enjoy the outdoor life, then it gives you the perfect excuse to forage for kindling. If you can obtain a tree that has been felled and chainsawn into logs, you can learn the best, most efficient way to split the logs then season them

Above: In contrast to an open fire, a woodburner is very easy to get started, it lets out a lot of heat quickly, and its output can be controlled and maintained easily.

Above right: Chopping wood for your woodburner is healthy, satisfying outdoors work and provides a good antidote to all the time we spend indoors sitting down.

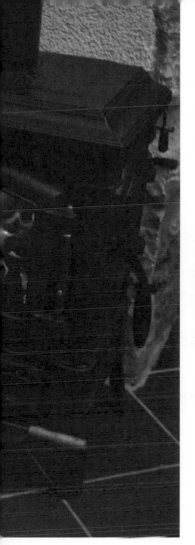

outdoors, under cover, ready to be used when they have dried. It is all very satisfying, and the exercise is good for you. Then, after a hard day's work in the open air, splitting and stacking logs, you can look forward to a long, hot soak in the bath, followed by relaxing in front of the very stove that was responsible for all that hard work in the first place!

If the outdoor life appeals to you, then buy a woodburner and make good use of it; it will repay your investment in time and effort many times over.

UNDERSTANDING
WOODBURNERS

How stoves **work**

A WOODBURNING STOVE IS AN ENCLOSED SYSTEM. It consists of a cast-iron or steel body, usually mounted on legs, with a glazed or solid metal door at the front and a flue exit on top or at the rear. Generally, there are vents or dampers above and below the door, with a means of opening and closing them. Inside there is a fixed grate (or a movable one, in the case of a multifuel stove), and below that the ash tray where ash is collected for disposal. The firebox has insulating bricks at the sides and a baffle plate above.

TIP

Check that the top of the flue is not obstructed. A big overhanging tree, for example, might prevent the smoke from escaping freely. This could result in smoke blowing back into the room when the stove is opened. If the flue exit is too low it may not draw well, because the air at that level is too still.

> The S-shaped airflow within the stove is much more efficient and controllable than an open fire, and results in a more predictable burn rate, producing less smoke.

The stove operates using a two-stage burning process (shown opposite), whereby air enters through the lower vents and passes through the firebox, fuelling combustion. The partially burnt smoke then passes under the baffle plate, where it stays hot, then burns for a second time before leaving via the flue (this is known as the secondary burn). The upper vents are used to control the burn rate. This S-shaped airflow is much more efficient and controllable than an open fire, and results in a more predictable burn rate, producing less smoke.

THE TWO-STAGE BURNING PROCESS

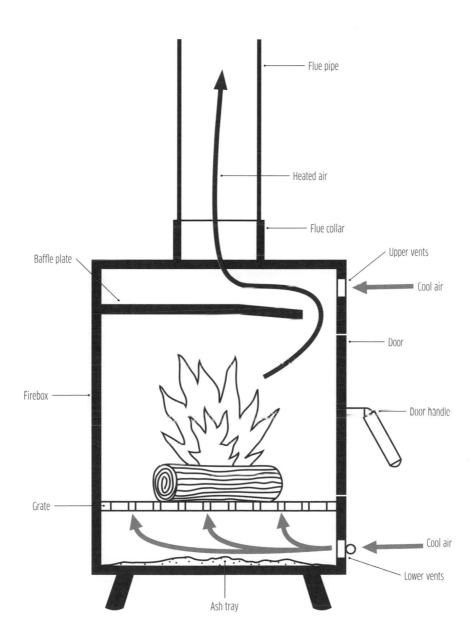

Flue pipe

Heated air

Flue collar

Upper vents

Baffle plate

Cool air

Door

Firebox

Door handle

Grate

Cool air

Lower vents

Ash tray

Location in the home

WHERE YOU LOCATE YOUR STOVE WILL MOST LIKELY play a part in dictating the size, style and features you go for. For instance, if you wish to place it in or near the kitchen, you might like to choose one that has a good cooking facility. If you have a large room, or are lucky enough to have a home or extension built to your own specification, then a model that is made to be seen all round could be sited right in the middle of the room. If you have a large, open-plan space, you'll probably want a stove with a large output to heat the area sufficiently. On the other hand, a small room will demand a small stove.

To understand this better, you need to consider how heat spreads from a stove. As the heat enters the air around the stove, it starts a convection current. As we all learned at school, heat rises, so the warmed air moves upwards. If you stand on a stepladder you will find a lot of very warm air up near the ceiling, where it isn't particularly useful; the process, like most conventional heating, is therefore inefficient. The hot air begins to cool and sink again, moving in a circulating pattern back towards the floor, ready to be heated again and move back up to the ceiling. The term 'convection' describes the whole of this circulation process – a continuous pattern over which we have little control. In addition, the stove and its flue will radiate heat – that is, release it into the room in every direction – so two heating effects, convection and radiation, are actually taking place at once.

TIP

Siting a flue exit at a lower level than a typical two- or three-storey house, or installing one in a property that did not previously have one, is quite likely to cause upset among neighbours and may contravene planning and building regulations. Check with neighbours first to see if they have any objections, and contact your local planning and building control departments.

Right: If your room has no chimney, this doesn't necessarily mean you can't have a woodburner; it may be that a rigid flue can be fitted through an external wall, or through the roof. You will need advice from a professional installer.

Because of the way warm air travels, you may find that the room with the stove in it will be very hot, while the room next door may be much cooler, even when the door between them is left open. To help counteract this, large vents can be inserted at the top and bottom of a dividing wall. Even better, if there are room dividers that can be opened back, this will allow the warm air to circulate. The ideal is to site the stove in an open-plan space, without internal walls or doors to restrict air movement around the ground floor and up to the first floor. If this is not possible, you can insert vents into ceilings to allow warm air to reach the floor above (subject to Building Control approval).

CIRCULATION FROM ROOM TO ROOM WITH VENTS IN DIVIDING WALL

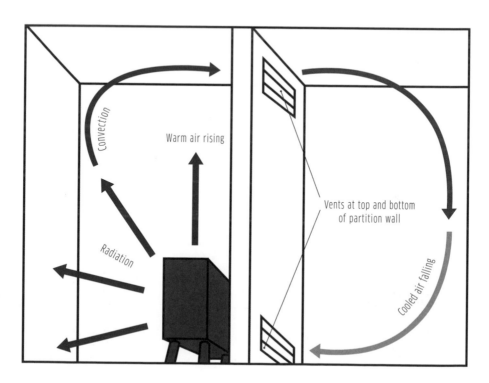

Convection

Warm air rising

Radiation

Vents at top and bottom of partition wall

Cooled air falling

CIRCULATION FROM FLOOR TO FLOOR
WITH VENTS IN CEILING

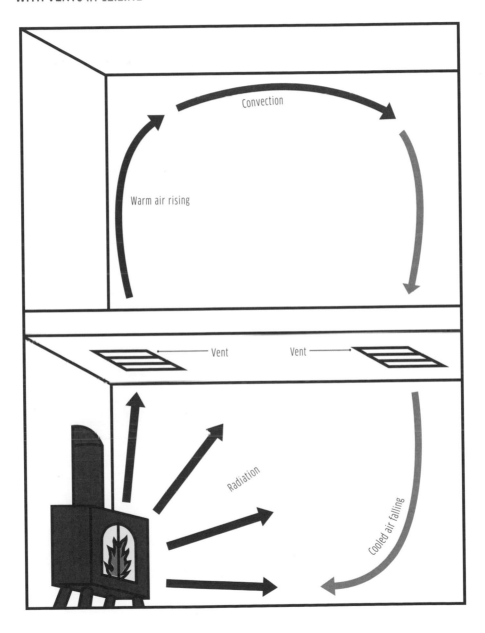

Choosing the right **size**

CONSIDER WHAT YOU ARE LOOKING TO GAIN FROM your stove. Do you wish it to heat your entire home? Will you be solely dependent on it for warmth? Or do you want it just to supplement your existing central heating, using the stove mainly for decorative effect?

In the latter case, it's worth bearing in mind the benefit of buying a stove that is big enough to cope in an emergency, should your primary heat source fail. It's reassuring to know that you have a backup if your central heating breaks down, or if it struggles to cope in extremely bad weather.

However, there is a downside to having a bigger stove. A large stove in a small room will be stifling. As a term of reference, a 5kW stove equates to two two-bar electric fires, which I think you would agree is quite a lot of heat output. Sitting by it in a small room will feel stifling to most people. Even if your room is very spacious, a large stove can still feel unpleasant if there isn't adequate ventilation in the room, particularly if you have double or triple glazing.

As a general rule, any woodburning stove above a 5kW output will require an additional air supply to feed it. You can have more airbricks inserted, or you can have window vents – but the latter would have to be permanently open, which is counterproductive in cool or windy weather when you are trying to keep the place warm. The best way, then, to avoid draughts is to have a special air feed, possibly under the floorboards, that vents in front of the woodburner.

TIP

The nominal heat output of a wood stove should be regarded only as a guide. The actual amount of heat produced will vary according to the vent settings, how clogged or clear the grate is, and the type of fuel being burnt. Much depends on how wet or dry the wood is. On a windy day the fire may draw faster, unless the vents are partly closed down to compensate. It's always worth taking professional advice before making your final choice.

Right: This stove is not large, but its heat output is perfectly sufficient for a modest-sized room. A larger stove might be overpowering.

As a rule of thumb, for every 14 cubic metres (14m³) of averagely insulated space you will need 1kW of heat to maintain a temperature of 22°C (70°F) when the outside temperature is 0°C (32°F). So you will need to work out the size of space you wish to heat, before you decide on the appropriate size of stove. If you're unsure, any reputable installer will be able to advise you on this.

SPACE CALCULATIONS

To measure cubic metreage, multiply the length and width of the room, then multiply that result by the height of the room. For example, if a room is 3.5m wide x 4m long, then the floor area is 3.5 x 4 = 14 square metres (14m²); if it's 3m high, then the volume is 14 x 3 = 42m³. If there are complications such as a boxed-in staircase, calculate the volume of the whole room first, then measure the boxed part and subtract that from the larger figure.

Even if you use your stove mainly for decorative effect, it's reassuring to know that you have a backup if your central heating breaks down, or if it struggles to cope in extremely bad weather.

Left: A large stove such as this provides sufficient output to heat an open-plan space with high ceilings. It also adds drama to a minimalist room.

Appearance and features

THERE ARE MANY FEATURES THAT CAN MAKE A STOVE more appealing. These can be functional, such as its method of venting (see page 22), its suitability for use in a smoke control area (see page 30) or its capacity for cooking (see page 10). They can also be more cosmetic, such as the colour or the size of glass you'd like in the door. Most importantly, you must decide whether you would like a stove that can burn multiple types of fuel, or one that is only suitable for woodburning.

A glazed door, or doors, will enable you to enjoy the look of the fire – and if it looks pleasing, that adds to the glow you will feel from the heat given out.

MULTIFUEL OR WOODBURNING
Quite apart from the 'green' aspect discussed on page 19, this is a no-brainer in my opinion. While it may be useful to have the capacity for changing fuel types, the likelihood is that you will stick to one; and the easiest to deal with is wood. Coal and smokeless fuels are dirty to handle and need storage that will contain the mess – in other words, a coal bunker. Wood can be stored in a number of ways that are easier to construct and arrange and still look reasonably presentable, or even impressive. I'm not sure I've ever heard anyone trying to impress visitors by the size of their coal bunker!

Right: A small antique stove like this would be an attractive feature in any room, but is unlikely to comply with modern safety standards.

Coal and smokeless fuels create a fused-together mess called clinker. Clinker needs a bit of effort to break up and remove before disposal (it can be put on an unmade driveway or in a dustbin (trash can) if there isn't too much of it). With woodburning, the ash tends to keep breaking down with each burning session and the loose ash will drop through the grate naturally. Care is needed in removal and disposal if you are to avoid a nasty spillage, but it's certainly easier than the alternative, in my experience.

SMOKE CONTROL AREAS

A well-maintained woodburner should produce less smoke than a coal fire. However, you may live in an area where the burning of conventional fuels is prohibited or restricted. In the UK these are commonly known as 'smokeless zones', and your local authority will be able to tell you whether you are in one. If you are, you will need to prove that your woodburner is suitable. If you choose a model approved by DEFRA (the Department for Environment, Food and Rural Affairs), you will be able to burn any fuels that are recommended for your stove, because these are specially designed to burn hotter and produce less smoke. Unfortunately, they tend to be more expensive. Alternatively, you can buy a standard stove, but in that case you'll be restricted to burning smokeless fuel (see page 47).

STEEL OR CAST IRON?

Many stoves are now being built from steel rather than the traditional cast iron. Steel stoves can be made lighter, so they do not take so long to warm up, and the welded construction gives an excellent air seal. Even if one of the welds should fail, it can usually be repaired. Steel construction is versatile and allows for more elaborate and imaginative designs.

Below: This steel stove has a sleek, modern look and takes up remarkably little floor space.

Cast iron, on the other hand, will continue to radiate heat for much longer than a steel stove. It is less prone to warping, and to corrosion from combustion products.

CHOICE OF DOOR

The style of doors is important. A glazed door, or doors, will enable you to enjoy the look of the fire – and if it looks pleasing, that adds to the glow you will feel from the heat given out. If you have the right space, you may wish to site your stove in the middle of the room, and this makes it worthwhile to have glass doors on both sides. A solid metal door is an option if you don't feel it necessary to observe or appreciate the fire in the grate, but I'm not aware of any great advantage in terms of cost or efficiency. Some double doors can be opened right back and left open while the stove is in operation – but do bear in mind that the heating efficiency drops in this mode, and safety is an issue because many species of wood tend to spit out sparks (see page 52).

Below: If you have the luxury of a large room and are able to place the stove in the centre of the space, it's worth choosing a model that is glazed on more than one side.

TECHNICAL TERMS

When you start looking for stoves, you may be confused by some of the technical or proprietary terms that you come across. Look for definitions on manufacturers' websites or discuss them with suppliers; however, here is a rough guide to some of the main terms you are likely to meet.

Airwash This feature is intended to keep the front glass clear (although I find it does depend on the correct use of the vents or dampers).

Back boiler or back box This refers to the built-in capacity to heat water in a radiator circuit.

Cleanburn stoves These are designed to minimize the amount of smoke produced. There are specific models that are approved for smoke control areas.

Convector stoves These release warm air through a special vent so as to encourage the formation of convection currents (see pages 20–23). You'll feel the heat from them more quickly than other stoves.

Preheating The flue will heat up quickly if the fire is burning rapidly. Once the burning process is established the fire needs to be damped; the flue will stay hot.

Primary and secondary air feed These terms are not always used consistently, but some manufacturers distinguish between a primary air feed, which is ducted into the stove from outside the building, and a secondary air feed, which is drawn from within the room. A well-insulated room that has been sealed against air leakage may not supply enough oxygen without the external feed.

Above: The curved lines of the door give this small stove a quirky, almost friendly look. You may come to think of it as one of the family!

WHAT STYLE DO YOU LIKE?

Woodburners are not only functional, they are decorative too. They come in many colours, shapes and sizes, from the very traditional to the ultramodern. The traditional styling is eternally popular and fits in surprisingly well with most modern interior decor by way of a contrast. Look in interior-design magazines to get ideas, then research what is available within your budget by checking online, ordering catalogues and visiting specialist dealers.

TIP

Having chosen your stove, you do not need to buy it straight away. You may be able to locate the same or a similar model elsewhere at a better price, or with lower delivery charges.

Accessories

YOUR STOVE SHOULD COME WITH THE FOLLOWING items, and if not, you will need to acquire them.

- A key or device for opening the stove door safely.
- A device for operating the riddling of the grate if it is a multifuel type.
- An ash-tray lifter to carry the ash tray safely and cleanly out and away from the woodburner for disposal.
- Special heatproof gloves with a rough texture to protect hands and forearms. I had to use mine recently when the baffle plate slipped down and jammed while the stove was alight. It was a crisis while it lasted – I had to remove burning wood and calm the fire down so I could lift out the hot metal plate and refit it correctly once the temperature in the stove had dropped sufficiently. So, always keep the gloves handy, just in case!

The following fire tools are also essential:
- Tongs, for retrieving glowing embers that occasionally fall out of the grate and for turning over logs to get them to burn on the other side while exposing a glowing face to the front.
- A small shovel for scooping up ash and tiny embers and placing them back in the grate.
- A natural-fibre brush for sweeping ash on to the shovel and tidying the hearth area. It has to be natural, not synthetic, so it cannot melt and will only scorch very slightly.
- A poker to prod logs into place and help break them down once they have burnt through.

Above and right: Carefully chosen accessories can be attractive furnishings in their own right. An elegant stand makes them look even more stylish, and is also a practical way of keeping them ready to hand for whenever you need them.

Methods of **installation**

FITTING A STOVE IS NOT DIFFICULT. THERE IS PLENTY of information online telling you how to do it. But you should not attempt it yourself unless you have the proper certificate. In the UK, HETAS (Heating Equipment Testing and Approval Scheme) is the official body that oversees training and certification for solid fuel and biomass heating. A HETAS Certificate is required by local authorities and buildings insurers in order to show that an installation was done safely and correctly. Don't take the risk of ignoring the need for certification. Installations should always be carried out to professional standards, and you should then have the protection of a certificate showing your installation meets the approved standard. A qualified professional will also advise you on the practicality of installation and the best method of achieving it, and on the choice of flue types. A professional installation can be completed in a day.

LOCATION
You must be sure to install your stove in a non-flammable environment that does not have any intrinsic hazard such as dust, gas or volatile elements floating around. The immediate area around the stove, flue and flue exit must be made of completely non-flammable materials: stone, concrete or whatever is classified as inert and safe. You need a good level of ventilation in the area where the stove is sited, both to feed oxygen to the woodburner and, most importantly, to ensure that you can breathe easily.

TIP

In theory, a woodburner should not affect anyone with breathing problems such as asthma, as it runs with doors shut and an enclosed flue. However, a certain amount of dust may be present in the atmosphere both during use and when removing ash. If you think this might be an issue for you, try visiting a working woodburner installation to see if it provokes a reaction, before committing yourself.

Right: This stove has been fitted against an existing chimney breast, but without using the original fireplace, which has been sealed. The flue pipe has been treated as a decorative feature.

USING AN EXISTING CHIMNEY

If you intend to use an existing chimney, then a qualified professional will need to check that it is suitable. It may be necessary to repoint or even rebuild an existing chimney stack and chimney before installing a flue lining. Any associated roof works are best done at the same time, by a professional builder.

Owners of open fires are always potentially at risk of a chimney fire, which can be quite alarming – literally, since you will have to call the fire brigade to put it out. With a woodburner the propensity for chimney fires increases greatly due to the more efficient, hotter burning process. Also, any leakage of carbon monoxide through brickwork could be a silent killer. Therefore a flue lining is obligatory for complete safety.

The flue lining is flexible, so it can be dropped down from roof level and pass any awkward bends or obstacles on the way down, such as a first-floor fireplace. A qualified installer will advise you on the correct lining diameter for the size of stove and the space available to accept it.

Professional installation of a flue lining will usually cost about double the price of an average woodburner, but it is well worth the money, as the installers save you the risk of working at height and will know how to get the flue into position properly.

The register plate

When the chimney is lined, the exit at the bottom is sealed off with a register plate; the last section of flue pipe, which is rigid and not concertinaed like the rest of it, will pass neatly through the register plate without any gaps. The bottom end of the pipe will locate in a collar on the top or back of the woodburner. Nowadays, the register plate tends not to be screwed into the

TIP

Before installation, your registered installer should sweep the chimney, for two reasons: to check for obstructions, and to remove messy and potentially flammable soot and other debris. Check with your installer that this process will be executed.

FLUE LINING INSTALLED IN AN EXISTING CHIMNEY

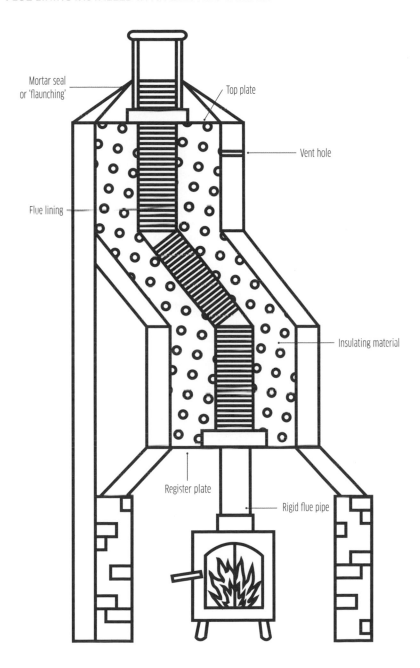

Mortar seal or 'flaunching'

Top plate

Vent hole

Flue lining

Insulating material

Register plate

Rigid flue pipe

fireplace masonry but bonded in place using a special high-strength builder's mastic. The flue fits tightly into the register plate and no seal is needed.

FITTING A RIGID FLUE PIPE

If you are not using an existing chimney, the alternative is a rigid flue pipe going through a wall or ceiling. Again, this is not a do-it-yourself job unless you have prior experience. The work must be done in accordance with building regulations, and if the flue is cranked it will need an access panel for sweeping. Installation is bound to involve disturbance of masonry and roof tiles or slates, so the work needs to be done in a way that doesn't cause major damage or compromise the weathering integrity of the building. If the flue passes through potentially flammable materials such as timber and insulation material, then it will need a heat-resistant collar around it to keep things safe. Where a flue exits through a roof, a weatherproof shroud will be needed to stop ingress of rainwater. There are special components available for these situations.

Above: The best types of cowl seem to be those with a cage-like grille around the circumference and a cap on top. When the flue is cleaned you'll be able to see the sweep's brush as it enters the cage.

A qualified installer will advise you on the correct lining diameter for the size of stove and the space available to accept it.

CAP OR COWL

The cap or cowl is the last bit on top of the chimney or rigid flue. It serves a couple of functions: it can keep rain out, and it will prevent birds nesting. It is not strictly necessary if rain doesn't drop down your chimney anyway, and if the flue is swept before use then birds' nests aren't a problem either. However, a cowl does give peace of mind on both counts.

RIGID FLUE PIPE INSTALLED WITHOUT AN EXISTING CHIMNEY

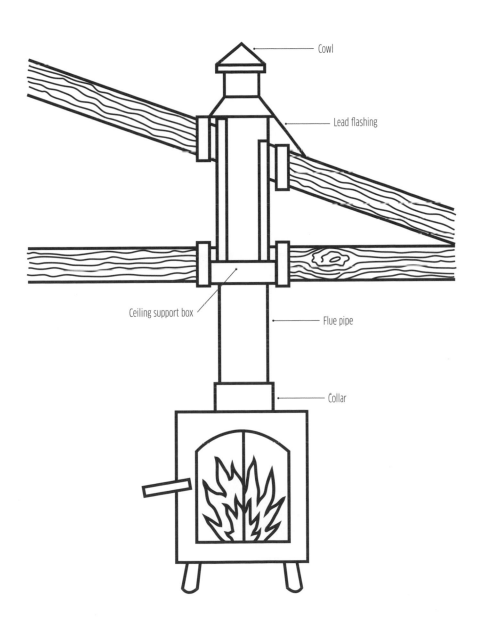

Cowl

Lead flashing

Flue pipe

Collar

Ceiling support box

FUEL
OPTIONS

Types of **fuel**

FOR ME, WOOD IS THE FUEL OF CHOICE. IT IS READILY available, relatively inexpensive, it burns well, can be stored easily, looks decorative, and is eco-friendly. However, you may own, or be considering, a multifuel stove. You may also live in a smoke control area and be restricted to smokeless fuels (see page 30). So, here is the low-down on the various fuel options that are available to you.

SPLIT LOGS

These are standard fodder for a woodburner, and are needed in great quantity if you are planning to use your stove a lot. You can buy them from a merchant or woodsman (see page 58). The purpose of splitting the logs is manifold. Unsplit, the bark will slow the drying of the wood, or even stop it from drying out properly, so splitting speeds the drying process greatly. Some of the best wood will come from large trunk slices that will never fit in the grate, so splitting several times will reduce them to manageable sizes. Bark acts as a sealer and insulator, so a whole round log cannot burn quickly because the bark is protecting it.

TIMBER OFFCUTS

I don't believe in waste. As a woodworker, waste wood is a fact of life, but when I'm having a clear-out of my timber store, or find that there are lots of odd ends of boards too short to be useful, it will all go for burning. It normally goes into a small, enclosed shed with ventilation so that it stays dry. Any species will do as far as I am concerned (but see the warning on allergies on the right), but the chunkier the sections the better, as these will burn slower and longer, which is preferable even though the calorific output is therefore reduced.

WARNING

Some exotic and temperate hardwoods are risky to handle, as skin contact and/or dust may cause an allergic reaction. If you have an allergy, or think you may have one, then handling wood of any kind could be a risk. Fine dust is the worst offender, as particles smaller than one micron can penetrate skin and lung tissue and can also irritate the throat and nasal passages. Teak dust, for example, can cause nosebleeds. Always wear appropriate PPE (personal protective equipment) if sawing and handling irritant timbers.

Note that the only legitimate reason for burning exotic or specialized woods is if they are workshop waste pieces or have been salvaged from a gutted property. No one burns such wood for its own sake, because it is too expensive – and many species will be on the CITES (Convention on International Trade in Endangered Species) list of banned timbers.

Right: If you are able to store some of your logs near the stove, this is an excellent way of reducing the moisture content of the wood before you use it (see pages 55–57).

ECO-LOGS OR BRIQUETTES

These are commercially produced artificial logs made by compressing sawdust, using the natural oils and resins in the wood dust as binders to hold them together. They are log-sized, sometimes solid, sometimes with a hole down the middle so that oxygen and flame can penetrate them from the inside to help them burn more efficiently. They work well and are an effective means of using a natural by-product of timber processing. Also, they have a consistent calorific output, which means good heating.

Above: Hardwood eco-logs will burn for longer than softwood, and only limited ash is created when burning.

There are two minuses, however. One is that they are expensive (though this reduces somewhat if you buy in bulk); the other is that they have to be kept 100% dry. If you don't do this, your store of reliable fake logs will crumble to dust, reducing their burning efficiency to near zero and likewise your financial investment in them.

I don't believe in waste. When I find odd ends of boards in my timber store that are too short to be useful, it will all go for burning.

COAL

Consisting of ancient trees, ferns and other vegetation compressed under successive layers of mud and rock under great pressure and at high temperature, coal is already 'half-baked'. Rather like charcoal, it contains vast amounts of carbon as well as atoms of hydrogen, oxygen and other elements. (Diamonds, oil and gas are all products of the same process.) It is classified as 'ancient carbon', which is a thing that concerns environmentalists greatly, since burning this material releases carbon into the atmosphere, contributing to global warming.

In addition, it is expensive and messy to handle and needs its own bunkerage to store it properly. It cannot be burnt in a standard woodburner, as you need to be able to riddle the grate (that is, rake it from beneath) to keep it clear; wood, on the other hand, burns best on a bed of ash and needs no riddling.

SMOKELESS FUEL

This is more acceptable than coal, as it has gone through a process to drive out the lighter hydrocarbon compounds that are normally released into the atmosphere when burning coal. This makes it less visibly polluting, but there are some lesser or invisible elements that still escape into the atmosphere. Storing the fuel requires a bunker, and clearing the grate of debris (known as clinker) isn't fun. Cost is an issue, too, and you will need a multifuel grate; but it is a handy standby, especially if you keep it tidily in the plastic bags in which it is supplied.

There are two categories of smokeless fuel: naturally smokeless anthracite (stove nuts) and manufactured types made from coke or anthracite. Ask your supplier which of the various brands is most suitable for your particular appliance.

NEWSPAPER BRIQUETTES

Newspaper briquettes are a labour of love. You create a wet block of compressed newspapers in a briquette maker, then leave it to dry. You will need time, plenty of newspapers and somewhere to store these soggy items while they dry out.

If you want to give them a go, the briquette maker is relatively inexpensive. Soak the newspaper in a bowl of water and leave it for a while for the fibres to soften and go fluffy. This will help the paper bind together. If you can spare it for a while, a bath with some water

Above: Smokeless fuel is more eco-friendly than coal, but it is still messy to use and less kind to the planet than burning wood.

Below: A newspaper briquette maker.

in is an excellent way to soak plenty of newspaper. Tear up the soggy paper into smaller pieces and push into the briquette maker until it is full, then pull down the handle to squeeze out the water. You may need to add more paper to make up the thickness and repeat the operation until the briquette is big enough to be ready to push out of the maker. Place it on a board to dry; a sunny day is best because you can dry a whole batch of briquettes outside. Clearly, you need to do this work well in advance of needing to use the briquettes, as it does take some drying time to do the job properly. Burning efficiency is similar to fast-burning logs.

Above: Rolled paper logs; there is more than one gadget on the market for making these. The more tightly wound they are, the longer they will burn.

PAPER LOGS

There are now one or two devices for dry-rolling paper into log 'rounds'; these are tightly bound together with wire, which is retrieved after burning. So long as these logs do not separate during burning, causing light ash to invade the neighbourhood, they seem to have useful potential for recycling.

KINDLING

To get your fire started, you will need kindling wood, which is smaller, more finely split sections of wood and twigs that are very dry and ready to burn. There's no need to buy kindling. You can pick it up off the ground in your local park or woodland. Maybe also, like me, you can generate some waste wood from doing DIY work. Trimming trees and bushes in your own garden can generate future kindling once it has had a chance to dry. Newspaper and plain cardboard are good to use alongside kindling wood, too. Dry moss is also good as kindling – minus the earth underneath, of course.

Right: Pine cones make good kindling and also look nice in a basket beside the stove. Going for a woodland walk and collecting pine cones can be a fun activity for all the family.

WHAT NOT TO BURN

It would be possible to give you a list as long as your arm of what isn't suitable for burning in a stove, so a certain amount of common sense must apply. However, a brief guide follows.

Plywood offcuts are not ideal, since the plies are sandwiched together with a resin glue that could cause some flue damage. I do not burn chipboard because it has such a high proportion of adhesive to sawdust. The same applies to MDF, which is wood dust glued together and contains formaldehyde, which again could be destructive.

I will burn old or recovered timbers that may have screws or nails in, with some exceptions. Some timber treatments are toxic and pollute the atmosphere, so I avoid anything that I know has a hazardous treatment. The same goes for very old painted wood, such as joinery ripped out from an old property, because earlier coats of paint, if they are original, will contain lead. Lead cannot break down or disperse and is very harmful to humans (and animals); it can cause developmental problems in young children, hence the use of unleaded fuel in vehicles today.

Woodburners are not intended to burn rubbish. Your local council will mostly likely be able to do this much more efficiently, using an incineration plant to create electricity from waste.

Cardboard for starting a fire, and newsprint in briquette form as fuel, are fine; however, most printed papers are coated with chemicals and do not burn so well, so they are far better sent for recycling. In any case, burnt paper will fly up the chimney and may cause annoying ash deposits for your neighbours.

TIP

I am disciplined about materials that can be burnt. Solid wood which is 'clean' can be cut up and burnt. Plywood waste gets burnt because there isn't too much resin but chipboard is a no-no because of the high chemical content. Likewise, painted or treated wood doesn't get burnt. Instead I take it to our local recycling centre for processing into chippings to make man-made board, etc. It isn't going to waste and it is making good use of what I can't burn, which is how it should be.

Natural or man-made fibre products such as fabric should not be burnt. Even though the former has much in common with wood, its rate of burn is far too rapid. Man-made material on burning behaves like any other plastic: it will burn far too fast and create a lot of toxic pollution, so it's a complete no-no.

Volatile substances such as paraffin oil, petrol (gasoline), white spirit (mineral spirit), cellulose thinners and paint must never, ever, ever find their way into a burning grate. Even a small amount dabbed onto a rag, for example, could be lethal. The possibility of a horrendous fire or even an explosion means these substances are completely unsafe. If you need to start a recalcitrant fire, or lift its spirits if it has sunk low in the grate with no glowing ember evident, then adopt a safe method such as firelighters – and use patience as well.

Above: This reclaimed timber may look like a promising source of fuel, but don't risk it – the paint is very likely to contain harmful lead.

Wood species

THE CHOICE OF WOOD SPECIES IS FAR LESS IMPORTANT with a woodburner than with an open fire. I know someone who uses a wood-fired boiler to heat the entire house: radiators, hot water and all. He coppices his own chestnut woodland. Chestnut, like pine, is frowned on by anyone with an open fire because of its propensity to spit sparks everywhere. That is not an issue with my friend's system, nor with a woodburner. Many of the timbers listed opposite do spit, but since the woodburner doors should be shut it shouldn't be a problem. If you must use your woodburner with the doors open, make sure you avoid the spitting species and use a fireguard.

Above: Because of the reduced risk of sparks, owners of woodburners can use a wider range of timbers than those who prefer an open fire.

Different fuels can be classified according to their calorific value, which is the amount of energy released by burning a fixed quantity of fuel; but for our purposes the comments given in the table may be more convenient.

Some timbers, mainly softwoods (woods from coniferous trees such as pine and spruce), burn quickly, so you will need more of them to get your fire going. Hardwoods (woods from broadleaved trees) generally last longer.

The drying times given in the table are for round logs split in half, then quartered and stored under dry, open cover. Drying times will approximately double for logs left in the round. But bear in mind that wood is a natural substance and not every piece will behave as you expect.

SPECIES	DRYING TIME	COMMENTS
Alder (*Alnus* spp.)	3 months	Burns fast; low-quality firewood
Apple (*Malus* spp.)	1 year	No spitting; must be well seasoned
Ash (*Fraxinus* spp.)	3 months	Best firewood; splits easily
Beech (*Fagus* spp.)	15 months	No spitting; must be well seasoned
Birch (*Betula* spp.)	6 months	Burns bright; bark is good firelighter
Cherry (*Prunus* spp.)	1 year	No spitting; must be well seasoned
Chestnut (*Castanea* spp.)	18 months	Spits; burns well
Hawthorn (*Crataegus* spp.)	1 year	Good firewood; burns well
Hazel (*Corylus* spp.)	1 year	Burns fast; no spitting
Holly (*Ilex* spp.)	1 year	Can be burnt part-seasoned
Hornbeam (*Carpinus* spp.)	1 year	Burns well
Larch (*Larix* spp.)	1 year	Splits; gives off oily residue
Oak (*Quercus* spp.)	18 months	Best firewood; burns slowly
Pine (*Pinus* spp.)	6 months	Burns rapidly; leaves oily soot
Sycamore, European (*Acer pseudoplatanus*)	1 year	Burns well
Willow (*Salix* spp.)	6 months	Burns fast, but season well
Yew (*Taxus* spp.)	18 months	Burns slowly

GREEN VS DRIED WOOD

Whatever species of wood you choose as fuel, it won't burn well or at a good rate if it is wet. A high moisture content slows down the burning process and reduces the calorific output, as more energy is expended drying the wood in the grate as it burns. It could also hasten wear to the flue pipe, meaning that it will need to be replaced sooner than expected.

Wood from a newly felled tree will be wet inside, unless the tree was already dead before felling. Trees depend on the water carried up from the roots, through the trunk and into the leaves and fruit via millions of tiny tubular cells. Deciduous trees (those that lose their leaves seasonally) will 'shut down' during winter months when it is cold. The cells cease to carry fluid and the tree effectively hibernates until spring. This is a good time to cut down trees, but it is not always convenient to wait, so felling generally takes place all year round. The result is wet wood – known as 'green' wood – which typically has a moisture content of around 50%. In an extreme case, I have experienced water running from the cut ends of a eucalyptus log like a leaking water tank. Wood in this condition is clearly not suitable for burning. So, whether it is bought or found, wood needs time and well-ventilated storage where it can dry, or 'season', sufficiently; otherwise we are just trying to burn water.

TIP

While hardwoods such as oak take a year or more to air-dry, pine can be ready in no more than six months. A limited amount of residual dampness will help to mitigate its rapid burn, which is caused by its fibrous nature and the oils and resins that it contains – these flare up nicely and boost its calorific output.

Wood dries quicker when split into smaller sections, so keep this in mind if you're wanting to speed up the drying process.

When you buy wood ready for burning, the seller should be honest about the degree of dryness. It will normally be 'air-dry', which means that it has been stacked and stored for months on end under dry, open cover, so that much but not all of the water has evaporated. This wood is likely to contain approximately 20% moisture and will have a substantially higher calorific value than green wood.

Above: Stages in firewood production, from whole logs to split kindling. Removing the bark will aid drying.

Left: You can purchase a moisture meter to check whether your wood is dry enough to burn. This is particularly useful if you are buying green wood or felling your own trees.

The problem isn't as bad as it sounds. If you store your wood properly (see pages 78–81) so it can stay dry – or start to dry out, if it was wet when you bought it – then eventually bring it indoors in small amounts, the house heat will do the final drying for you and reduce the moisture level yet further. Also, wood dries quicker when split into smaller sections, so keep this in mind if you're wanting to speed up the drying process.

It is worth noting that carpenters, joiners and furniture makers require kiln-dried timber, which may have as little as 8% moisture, and wood as dry as this has maximum calorific value. So, if you can get your hands on offcuts – provided they have not been treated with anything that might cause a fire hazard – then they will burn very well alongside your split logs.

'Air-dry' timber has been stacked and stored for months on end under dry, open cover, so that much of the water has evaporated.

Finding a log supplier

IT'S A TRICKY BUSINESS FINDING A LOG SUPPLIER. There are a number of sources, but how do you know who to trust? The old saying 'you get what you pay for' is as true for logs as it is for anything else. A bargain price for a 'load' of wood (see page 60) probably isn't a bargain after all. The timber could be damp inside, there will probably be unsorted species and awkward, unusable sizes. Once it's sitting in a massive mound on your front driveway, you'll begin to wonder if you might have made a mistake. But the supplier won't be interested in taking it all back after he's got your money! In this situation, the best you can do is to chop anything down that's oversize and put it in long-term ventilated storage to dry out.

Above: It can be cheaper to buy a load of unprocessed timber if you are able to chainsaw it, split it and then store it yourself. However, it is important to note that chainsawing is a skilled technique and full training must be given first. It should never be attempted by novices.

In any case, can you tell whether it is good wood? Most of us struggle to identify standing trees, let alone those that have been felled and cut into unrecognizable slices.

So, to be sure of what you are getting, it is important to choose a supplier who has a good reputation. They won't be the cheapest, but, more importantly, they will be honest with you. They should be able to tell you what they are supplying, which will often be a mixed load of oak, ash, etc.; this is fine, as these species are good for burning. They should also be able to give you a rough idea of how dry the timber is.

The best way to find a reputable timber supplier is by word of mouth. A good starting point is talking to friends and acquaintances who already buy split logs for their own open fires or woodburners. Woodburners are far less fussy than open fires, so if the stuff is good for an open fire then you can be sure it will be

Right: This trailer load of wood has been split into wedges ready for burning.

good for your purposes. The next best thing is to find adverts in local papers and on the Internet. Make sure you understand what they are supplying in terms of quantity and types of wood and its condition.

Logs inevitably vary in size – wood is a natural product, so size and shape aren't constant. However, the key thing is that logs must not be too long to fit in the firebox. They can always be split down the grain if they are too wide, but shortening them is hard work, so ask your supplier to give you sizes suitable for your woodburner. It is useful to have some smaller pieces that come between kindling and split-log size; you can use them to help get a fire going, or to restart it if it has gone dull and needs a bit of encouragement.

TIP

One thing you don't want to do is buy a small bag of log wood from your local store or petrol station. It won't get you very far at all and will most likely go up in smoke in a couple of hours.

Ask your supplier to specify how many cords, cubic feet or cubic metres his load consists of. He should be able to tell you, or at least give you a very good approximation.

WHAT IS A LOAD?

Traditionally, log wood was sold in 'cords' – a cord being a quantity of timber, well stacked and arranged, equating to a contained stack 8 x 4 x 4ft, or 128 cu ft (3.6m^3) in volume. At one time this made sense, but this is too precise and sensible for the modern world! You are most likely to be promised 'a load'. This could mean anything: a trailer load, a builder's rubble-sack load, a truckload even. Ask your supplier how many cords, cubic feet or cubic metres his load consists of. He should be able to tell you, or at least give you a very good approximation.

Right: These logs have been cut into usable sizes, but now need to be brought under cover so they can dry out.

Foraging for wood

Above: Dry sticks gathered on a woodland walk make excellent kindling. The children can get involved, too. And if you spot some moss, then pick that up as well – once the earth beneath it has been removed it also makes for good kindling. There is no need to pay for kindling!

ONE THING YOU CAN DO ANY TIME YOU GO FOR A WALK or drive in the countryside is to look for wood to forage and bring back home. There is, however, the issue of land ownership and whether you have any right to remove fallen timber for burning. This will vary according to where you live; in the UK, generally speaking, there is no such legal entitlement, so if you happen to see the odd dead branch lying on the ground and decide to remove it discreetly, be aware that you could be challenged.

Usually, where there are forests there are special rights given to people living in the forest, and these may include the right to remove a certain amount of wood for their own use. Therefore, if you happen to see someone loading up a trailer with fallen branches, don't assume you have the right to do the same, as they may well live in the forest. On the other hand, you may get to know a landowner who is quite happy for you to tidy up his land a bit by getting rid of nuisance branches and fallen trunks. I've often found that if I mention to someone during the course of a conversation that I own a woodburner, it sparks a train of thought and I then get offered some wood to burn.

Let's assume you have legitimately found some branch wood for burning. You need to consider whether it's worth scavenging. Is it quite solid and heavy, or is it very light and rotted through? If the timber hasn't much substance to it, there may be little point in retrieving it, as it won't last five minutes in the grate.

Is it solid but covered in mud? This is better, but the mud needs to go. The wood will be messy to move, and you'll need a polythene sheet or tarpaulin to protect the

Right: Fallen timber may look inviting, but don't assume you have a right to take it without asking. This woodland looks as though it has been left to nature, but the chances are that it has been carefully managed to give this effect.

Left: It is worth buying a good-quality pruning saw with ultra-sharp teeth for efficient cuts.

boot (trunk) of your car. You will also need to wear old clothes in case you get mud everywhere. Then, of course, once the wood is brought home you need to get rid of the mud by washing it off. Mud that is left on can go iron-hard or get stuck in the bark structure. All this is a bit of a nuisance but may be worth it if you have a place where you can leave it to dry ready to cut up and burn.

Once you have located some usable timber, you will need to go suitably equipped with protective clothing against the elements, and safety footwear. A decent pruning saw can handle moderate branch sizes. You can then cut found branch wood to length or remove side branches so it will fit in your car. The roof rack may be an option. Branches are rarely straight, so it may be difficult to strap them safely in place. You may be able to slide long branches up between the front seats, so long as they are stowed safely and don't interfere with your ability to drive the car.

Once you have got your new-found treasure home, a couple of criss-cross log-horses will hold the branches one at a time while you cut them into short lengths with a pruning saw or bow saw. If you know someone who is qualified to use a chainsaw, ask nicely and they may cut it all up for you. But don't be tempted to use a chainsaw yourself unless you have been properly trained and hold the appropriate certificate.

Right: The simplest of saw-horses will hold your timber while you cut it to length.

Owning **woodland**

IMPROBABLE THOUGH IT MAY SEEM, IT IS ENTIRELY possible to buy your own piece of woodland. You don't need to be a big landowner, and if you have some money tucked away you might just be in a position to purchase a plot without breaking the bank.

As you might imagine, the trees don't fell themselves; there is a whole long process to growing, cropping and turning the wood into usable logs. The trees need to be the right species to be worth burning. The parcel of land needs to be in a good position so the trees will grow healthily and the soil drains properly and doesn't get waterlogged. You need to be trained in using a chainsaw safely, and you will need a trailer and a suitable towing vehicle. It's not for everyone, but I know of several people who have found it a worthwhile investment, and no longer have to rely on log suppliers at all.

There are, of course, legal responsibilities that come with owning woodland. You need permission to fell trees, unless you are coppicing, which causes multiple regrowth of new tree trunks. You cannot live on the land for more than 28 days at a time, so only temporary structures such as a tent or caravan are allowed, and you cannot run a business on the site. It is advisable to buy from a business that specializes in selling parcels of woodland with support and advice. There are organizations that help potential buyers and sellers of woodland, and they can advise on all aspects of purchasing and ownership.

TIP

There are a number of companies that deal in the sale of woodland, and they can give you a lot of help and advice. Websites belonging to the Forestry Commission and charities such as the Woodland Trust in the UK (and similar organizations in other countries) offer impartial advice and information. One of the best ways to access advice is to visit an agricultural show, where there is usually at least one stand that deals with matters such as buying woodland. You then get to chat face to face with someone who can explain things in detail. You are under no pressure to buy, and they should be able to answer questions about what type of woodland is suitable, and the legal implications of ownership.

Right: Owning a piece of land like this may not be as unlikely as you think – but do keep in mind the responsibilities that come with landowning.

HOW MUCH LAND DO YOU NEED?

The size of a parcel of land will depend on many things. How much money have you got to spend, including any legal fees? Is the land heavily wooded, or rather poor forestry soil? Does it have firebreaks, rights of way, streams, rock formations or any other factors that make it less than ideal? What kinds of trees are currently growing, and how mature are they? Are there protection orders on any of the trees? Are the trees native to the area ideal for burning? A specialist woodland business can guide you to the right decision. You will usually find that a set parcel of land has a set price which you can either accept or not.

HOW QUICKLY DOES WOODLAND REGENERATE?

Some species will regenerate quickly; birch is an example. Oak, however, will take vastly longer to mature, and may therefore be protected and not available for cropping.

Above: Coppiced trees are easily recognized by the multiple slender trunks growing from a single 'stool'.

As an example, paper birch reaches maturity in about 60–70 years but is usable for firewood at 40 years. That is a relatively fast-growing tree, so you can see there is no quick fix if you need firewood all the time. Good silviculture practice covers such things as how far apart trees should be spaced, regeneration by sprouting (for species such as hazel) or seeding (as with birch), and whether clear felling of a site is needed for saplings to thrive. It is well worth seeking professional advice on what is undoubtedly a complicated subject.

COPPICING

Coppicing is the ancient and universal practice of felling a tree while leaving the lowest section (the 'stool') so new shoots can sprout from it. It avoids killing a tree and allows useful wood products to be grown and cropped as a result. Birch, for example, can be cropped

on a three- to four-year cycle for brushwood called faggots, while mature oak trees can be cropped at about 50 years to create firewood. Coppiced wood has many practical uses, such as hurdle- and basketmaking, but is not really suitable for firewood.

LEGAL MATTERS

With land ownership come responsibilities. If you do intend to buy a parcel of woodland, make sure you get relevant legal advice first. Quite apart from the transaction itself, you must be aware of other matters such as protection of trees where appropriate, keeping rivers and streams clean, allowing access on public footpaths, and protection of various species of wildlife – which, incidentally, includes wild flowers as well as birds, bats and mammals. It is not only an offence to burn unapproved fuels in smokeless zones, but also to knowingly sell wood to someone living in a smokeless zone, unless they have a stove that is exempted because it emits very little smoke.

WARNING

Chainsaws are lethal in the wrong hands. If you want to use one to fell your own trees and cut them to burnable length, the only option is to undergo a proper training course. It should not be possible for you to buy or hire a chainsaw without a licence. You will also need to wear the correct protective equipment.

How to **chop wood**

THIS IS HARD PHYSICAL WORK, WHEN DONE THE traditional way with a splitting maul. One side of the maul's head is like a sledgehammer, the other like an axe. It usually has a hook at the back for helping to separate split wood.

You can either strike wood using the axe side, or use the sledgehammer side to drive in a splitting wedge or a 'log grenade'. The latter option is generally used when splitting logs with a large diameter.

You need a large slice of log to use as your 'anvil' on which to place each log you want to split. It must not rock, but sit solidly on the ground. Once the tip of the splitting wedge or log grenade is in the log, the splitting maul can be raised and brought down smartly on the top of it with some force. With practice, you will be able to land a blow without missing almost every time.

Above: Splitting a log with a sledgehammer and a 'log grenade'. Note the 'anvil' log placed beneath the log being split.

A sharp edge is not required; blunt force works better.

Should the log you are trying to split become stuck on the blade, rather than levering it off it is better to lift splitter, log and all, and bring them down hard on your chopping block so the wood is forced to split apart. Never raise them above your head! I find using a rather blunt log grenade gets around this problem because the maul is always free to use – only the grenade gets stuck in the log, and repeated blows will make the log give up and fall apart.

Left: Clockwise from top are two splitting wedges, a splitting maul, a 'log grenade' and a sledgehammer.

If you use a splitting axe or the splitting edge of a maul, it's worth noting that a sharp edge is not required. This may seem to run counter to the usual idea that a cutting edge should be sharp, but what is required here is blunt force. It works better, and you don't need to worry about laborious sharpening sessions.

There are also manual, electric and petrol (gasoline) log splitters, which make the job safer and easier. Of course, the electric model is no use unless you are near a mains supply, but if you intend to do a lot of log splitting yourself, a petrol model may be a good investment.

Right: A hand axe can be used as an alternative to the maul or sledgehammer and wedge.

USING WEDGES TO SPLIT A LOG

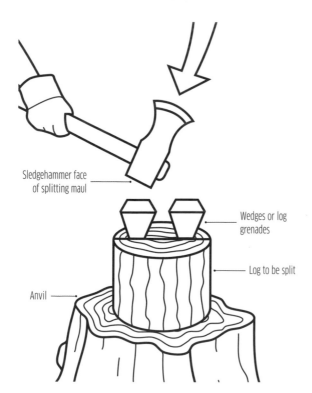

Sledgehammer face of splitting maul

Wedges or log grenades

Log to be split

Anvil

TIP

Two splitting wedges are often better than one. Drive each one alternately until the wood gives way. If one wedge gets stuck, the other can be used to retrieve it.

Log splitting may be a strenuous activity, but it need not be dangerous if sensible precautions are taken:

- Whichever tools you use, you will need the correct clothing and safety footwear. You will need safety goggles, a pair of leather armoured gloves, and safety boots with steel toecaps and sole inserts. When splitting logs you need to prepare properly before starting. Do not start work without the proper safety wear and sensible work clothing.
- Do some warm-up exercises such as touching toes, running on the spot, etc., to warm and loosen muscles before exerting yourself.
- You will get hot after a while, so keep a bottle of water or soft drink handy to avoid dehydration, and a towel to wipe your brow. I like to wear proper work trousers but just a T-shirt, so I don't get overheated and sweat too much.
- Check that the head of your maul or axe is secure. Modern ones often use a bonded construction which should be very safe.
- Make sure no one else is in your swing line, so they cannot get hit, and that there are no other obstacles.
- Do not bother with half-hearted swings, which can be difficult to control. I make very measured blows standing quite calmly and striking resolutely – don't get angry with the wood!
- Try to avoid striking ahead of the log or behind it. If you stand with the maul head resting comfortably on the log (as shown opposite), that shows the distance from which you should hit the log.
- To avoid back damage, work at improving your aim, so you strike where you intended to rather than bouncing off to one side.

TIP

Pace yourself when log splitting – don't try to rush through a large quantity as you'll likely tire more easily and be susceptible to making errors. Follow the advice given, but also accept that over time you will find a method and choice of equipment that works best for you. To a great extent, the tree or logs will determine how best to work because some will split easily and others will defy you, especially when you find the maul or splitting axe is buried close to a large, hard knot and cannot be extracted without great expenditure of effort. Try to 'read' each log and find the straightest path through without knots or branches before taking aim.

CORRECT STANCE FOR SPLITTING WOOD

Make a steady downward strike. Do not lift the axe above your head.

Safety goggles

Armoured gloves

Steel toecap boots

How much wood do you need?

THERE ISN'T A HARD AND FAST RULE FOR CALCULATING your fuel needs. It can vary tremendously depending on a number of factors: the size of your woodburner, its working efficiency, how much you use it and the kinds of wood you burn. Softwoods burn quickly, so you'll get through a lot; hardwoods burn slowly so will last you longer. (See page 53 for more information on different types of wood and their properties.)

If you mainly rely on central heating and only use your woodburner to make a room more pleasant and inviting at weekends, then you won't need lots of wood. This is fine, of course, until there is a power failure and your heating system is unable to run. That's when you will wish you had a lot more seasoned split wood waiting to be burnt – suddenly trying to acquire firewood when supplies may be limited can be expensive. Buying and storing well ahead can spread the cost, and it will be instantly ready to use. It is that reassurance that makes it worth doing.

At the other end of the spectrum I know of a young couple with a child who use only a woodburner to heat their home in the winter months, including radiators and hot water. In a particularly cold spell, they can get through a ton of wood in a month.

Ultimately, you will need to develop an eye for how long it will take your woodburner to go through a given quantity of fuel at an average or exceptional burn rate. In time this will become second nature.

TIP

A stove that is plumbed in to radiators will demand a lot more wood than one that isn't.

Above: Stacking split logs to dry in the open air. Note the dry hardstanding on which the logs are piled, and the poles that will support a waterproof cover to protect the logs from the worst of the weather.

Stacking and storing logs

FIRST, AND MOST IMPORTANTLY, YOU WILL NEED dry, ventilated storage. Anything less than that and your efforts will be wasted. Timber that stays damp or gets damp is harder to burn. It becomes covered in fungus and woodlice, and may even harbour voracious woodborers such as the woodboring weevil.

You might think that fully enclosed storage would be best, but in fact the ideal is a top cover to keep off the worst of the weather, leaving the front of the stack open to the elements so the air can get through and carry off moisture as the wood dries. Logs should be kept off the ground so they stay dry and don't start to rot, and the stack needs to be neat and stable with a uniform airflow throughout it. For wet weather, a drop-down tarpaulin can be used to shield the wood and carry off the rainwater; but hitch it up neatly out of the way in better weather so moisture cannot get trapped under cover.

There are different designs of storage and you will need to decide what is practical in your own situation. The best kind, though, is a stack placed away from any walls so the air can get around it easily. This type of stacking can be done in rows or aisles if you have the room, so you can move between rows to stack or remove logs. The more usual arrangement, however, is a lean-to store against a wall, with a slanting roof to let rainwater run off. This doesn't give the same level of ventilation but is perfectly adequate.

TIP

The smart thing is to build or adapt every practical space you can outdoors to take log storage. Start buying or collecting wood at least a year before you need it. If you are new to wood burning, use wood waste and eco-logs for now but build up a long-term store of split logs that can do their final drying ready for the next burning season.

Right: Logs drying under cover. This log pile boasts the luxury of a permanent roof.

The real problem with log storage is not having nearly enough of it. Anything you can do to increase the space will help, as you can then buy wood when it is readily available and possibly cheaper, and ensure that it is dry and ready to burn when you need it. It's also a good idea to have a small stack of logs indoors so that the ones you are about to burn have a chance to dry out a little more before you use them.

Above: A lean-to store with a wooden roof helps to keep logs dry.

Left: A less permanent but equally effective arrangement; note how the logs are raised off the ground to protect them from moisture rising from below.

USING AND
CARING FOR
YOUR STOVE

Lighting the stove

THE FIRST TIME YOU LIGHT A WOODBURNER FROM new, allow it to burn slowly to give it a chance to settle down – the cast iron, fire cement and insulating firebricks all need a chance to 'bed in'. You will need plenty of ventilation too, because fumes may be emitted from the metal and other components for a couple of days. These by-products of the manufacturing process smell unpleasant and could cause headaches, so make sure windows are left partly open until the fumes dissipate. Grate polish or other surface treatment can also give off fumes during a new burn.

Take single sheets of newspaper, screw them into balls and pop them in the empty grate. They will spring open a bit, but this does not matter. Their job is to give you something to light to start with. Since they are thin and very dry, oxygen can feed the flame given to the paper by a match very easily and they will burn up before you know it. Alternatively, you can use firelighters.

Ensure both top and bottom air vents are open so there is no restriction to air moving through the stove. On top of the many screwed-up balls of newspaper, place some kindling wood. I tend to place it criss-cross on the bed of paper, so there is space underneath in the middle to reach the paper to ignite it. The flame will lick upwards and catch the kindling.

Light your match then apply it not just to paper in the centre of the grate but elsewhere too before the match burns out. I generally get it to light in three places before chucking the match into the grate. This should be enough to ignite the kindling.

TIP

Note that when you first use your woodburner you will have a completely empty grate, which is not what a woodburner likes. A bed of ash to sit wood on works far better because it restricts airflow in a positive way and creates a 'hotbed' underneath freshly placed wood. Of course, even further down the line you won't always be able to avoid a clear grate, as a clear-out is required every now and then when the ash level rises too much and restricts the space for new wood.

1 *Bringing dried kindling to the grate, which already has a layer of newspaper on it.*

2 *Kindling stacked in alternate directions to allow air to circulate through and beneath it.*

3 *Lighting the paper. Be sure to light it in more than one place, as it will not necessarily catch at the first attempt.*

4 *Now the kindling is alight, it is time to part-close the door to encourage the Venturi effect (see next page).*

5 *Let the fire take hold of the kindling and burn fiercely before adding split logs.*

GETTING THE FIRE GOING

The next thing is to nearly close the door, just leaving
it slightly ajar. The reason for this is to create a Venturi
effect. This well-understood physical phenomenon
is what results by restricting airflow – it causes the
airflow to actually speed up. This might not seem logical
but it works, and it will help the kindling catch alight.
At this stage you can't leave the fire alone, because
it is young and weak and needs a little bit of work
to complete the job. Once the paper and kindling are
properly alight and you can see the kindling glowing in
parts along its edges, you'll need to put some 'proper'
sections of wood on the fire. These need to be placed
so they don't snuff out the young fire beneath.

*Above: Success! This is what
you should see once the fire is
established. Partly closing the
vents will cause it to burn more
slowly and evenly.*

You need split pieces of log wood with narrow edges that can catch alight easily. Round, bark-covered logs won't burn so readily. Leave the door slightly open as before, then once the fire seems to have embedded itself a bit you can close it securely.

Above: It is worth buying extra-long matches. They can reach right to the back of your woodburner and are much safer and easier to use than the standard sort.

One advantage of a glazed door is that you can not only enjoy watching the flames safely behind glass and appreciate the process that is taking place, but you can also judge how well the fire is working. Once you can see the bright yellow glow of the wood burning, it is time to close the lower vents down a bit to restrict airflow. Closing them completely would remove too much oxygen and result in incomplete combustion, which would release more pollutants into the atmosphere and cause tarring in the flue. So let enough air in to allow combustion and enough to allow the lighter elements to burn and escape up the flue. Every stove and its settings are different, and getting this balance right requires a bit of trial and error. In time, you'll get the knack just right for your stove.

When the vents are fully open, the fire will usually burn bright yellow in the grate. Once the vents are partially closed, the bright high peaks of yellow flame die down and a more even burn takes place. If there is a good bed of ash with a large log sitting in it, the log will tend to take on an orangey red glow; the ash prevents it from burning through quickly, like kindling.

With a glazed door, you can not only enjoy watching the flames safely behind glass and appreciate the process taking place, but you can also judge how well the fire is working.

Maintaining a fire

HAVING GOT A FIRE WORKING WELL, YOU NEED TO rebuild the fire enough to maintain it for a longer period. Using well-seasoned, quality logs will help to ensure this. What you are looking for is a good bed of ash in the grate, on top of which are hot, red, glowing embers. A tap with a poker will break these up a bit and spread them out. Now lay a new log or logs on top and close the door. Try to place new logs towards the back of the stove where it burns hotter, and place them lengthways so that any spitting from the end grain of the wood doesn't splatter onto the glass. The grate should never be overfilled: if you jam too much wood in, the baffle plate will get dislodged. Only if the fire doesn't seem to pick up after a while should you riddle the grate to let a bit more air up through it; otherwise, just leave it to burn slowly.

Above: Breaking up and spreading out the embers in preparation for laying fresh logs on top.

Experiment with the air-vent settings: the lower vent will feed the fire with oxygen, while the upper one will encourage the secondary burning process (see pages 18–19). Completely closing both vents will stifle the fire and cause tarring of the flue. Note that the lower-placed air inlet is usually part of an 'airwash' feature, partly designed to create a flow of cool air from outside up the back of the glass. This promotes the burning of carbon-producing elements which would otherwise darken the glass, and thus hopefully keeps the glass clear. If you completely close this vent the fire may smoulder, but it will also pump out more pollutants and the glass will blacken. Any wood lying close to the glass is likely to cause carbonization, too. It's good to keep the glass clear as much as possible, not only because it looks nicer but also because this saves you the job of cleaning it too often (see page 96).

Right: A brightly burning fire seen through clean glass – what could be cosier?

Overnight fires

These might seem like a good thing, but you need to keep the fire at a low ebb, which isn't so good as far as burning efficiency is concerned. When the weather is really cold I top up the fire late in the evening to give it a 'last blast' before we all go to bed. However, too much heat in the air can make the atmosphere overly dry and uncomfortable when everyone is asleep, so it is generally better to let the air cool a bit. You can always throw on a thicker duvet or blanket, and in any case cooler air will be better for anyone with nocturnal breathing issues, especially with a cold or flu.

The other advantage of letting the woodburner run down overnight is that once it has gone out you can safely riddle the grate in the morning and empty the ash pan if necessary. I tend to do this once a week. It's a chance for a fresh start and will have allowed the oxygen levels throughout the house to regenerate. You need the fire, but remember that the fire also needs air, which you both share.

When smokeless fuels are used, the grate should be riddled and the ash pan emptied every morning because of the build-up of clinker which inhibits airflow around and beneath the grate.

Above: Ash needs to be removed about once a week, and allowing the fire to burn out makes it much easier to do this.

Your woodburner's efficiency drops quite heavily when the doors are open, because effective operation relies on the higher rate of airflow caused by the circuit inside the stove once the door, or doors, are shut.

IMPROVING HEAT FLOW

All woodburners work largely by convection (see pages 20–23), but those that are described as convector stoves are the most efficient at distributing heat, because they are specifically designed to vent warm air in a way that encourages the formation of convection currents, in addition to radiating heat. But whatever type of stove you have, there are several things you can do to improve heat flow.

Always use your stove with the doors closed. Its efficiency drops quite heavily when they are open, because effective operation relies on the S-shaped burning path described on pages 14–15, and the higher rate of airflow caused by the circuit inside the stove once the door, or doors, are shut.

Try using a bimetallic fan. This natty little device simply sits on top of your woodburner and uses the stove's heat to provoke a reaction in the metal of the fan base; this creates enough electricity to drive the small fan. It is intended to push warm air from the stove out into the room for extra benefit. It may seem like a gimmick, but it really does work. If you put your hand in front you can feel the warm air being pushed forward instead of simply travelling upwards. For a fairly minimal cost, it is well worth considering buying one.

On a few types of stove that have a suitable top profile with a ledge, you may be able to enhance the radiating effect by neatly wiring a group of completely open tin cans around the top to increase the heat distribution area – not elegant, but surprisingly effective.

Above: This small fan costs nothing to run because it is powered by the heat of the stove. Place it towards the front of the stove so heat is drawn in from behind. Don't run the stove so hot that the fan gets damaged.

Above: Open tin cans strapped to a stove to increase heat distribution.

SAFETY POINTS

Safe practice is always important where fire is concerned, so here are a few safety caveats to be observed.

Carbon monoxide

If your stove is installed incorrectly, or in a room without enough ventilation, there is a risk of incomplete combustion, which emits toxic gases into the air. Carbon monoxide is an odourless, poisonous gas that is released into the atmosphere during combustion with inadequate ventilation. It can cause death as well as serious long-term health problems, so it is not something to take lightly. That is why a carbon monoxide detector is essential to operate a woodburner safely. They are inexpensive and easy to install.

To make sure it is working correctly, there is a test button that should be pressed once a week or so. An ear-splitting shriek will tell you that it is working. A carbon monoxide detector can be fixed or simply placed in a suitable location, preferably quite high up, where circulating air will waft across it. One detector in the room where the woodburner is situated is the bare minimum. It should be kept free of dust that might reduce its effectiveness.

Avoiding a chimney fire

Regular sweeping is essential (see pages 102–5). A chimney liner does not protect you from a chimney fire. It's advisable to have your chimney swept twice a year if burning wood, and once a year if using smokeless fuel.

WARNING

In the unlikely eventuality of your stove causing a house fire, do not throw water on the stove itself if it is made of cast iron, as this could cause a hot cast-iron stove to explode. Instead, throw water on the surrounding areas that are alight.

Correct operation and maintenance

The woodburner should be operated in accordance with the manufacturer's instructions and not modified in any way. The firebricks inside need to be in good order. Occasionally one will crack, but so long as it is pushed tightly together it will last a while until replacement. Likewise the top baffle plate needs to be correctly positioned, and the stove should not be operated without it in position. The fireproof seal or 'fire rope' around the door needs to be checked regularly and replaced when it becomes badly frayed (see pages 100–1). Cracked door glass must also be changed to ensure the fire chamber is sealed safely.

Above: A fireguard is essential if you like to have the doors open on your woodburner. It also protects small children and animals from touching the stove when it is hot.

Fireguard

Leaving the door of a woodburner open reduces its burning efficiency. If you do choose to do so, then not only do you need a fireguard in place, but the stove should not be left unattended for any length of time. Leaving it open while you leave the premises overnight is inviting disaster.

Burns

Kneeling in front of a woodburner to refill it carries a risk of accidentally pitching forward onto a very hot stove. The immediate tendency is to put out a hand to save yourself, but NOT on the stove itself, as a serious burn could result. Should you have the misfortune to get burnt, the only quick remedy is to place the damaged skin straight under a running cold-water tap and keep it there. Don't be tempted to stop this emergency treatment too soon, as your skin and flesh will have received a massive dose of heat which the cooling effect of the water takes some time to remove. You will need to phone for emergency medical assistance if the damage is severe. There are creams and dressings available that are suitable for minor surface burns; it's a good idea to keep some in the house.

Looking after your stove

YOUR WOODBURNER SHOULD BE YOUR PRIDE AND joy, so it is worth looking after it and keeping it in tip-top condition. This isn't onerous; it just needs to be done every now and then as the need arises.

CLEANING THE CASING

Most woodburners have cast-iron cases that look great straight out of the packing case, but use makes them a bit dull and dusty. There are various stove-cleaning agents you can try. I use grate polish, which is a thick, graphite-based paste that is rubbed on and buffed off to give a graphite-black sheen. This is a job I do probably only once a year when the burning season has finished, because a running stove burns off the grate polish, which doesn't smell very pleasant.

Above: For enamelled or steel stoves, baking soda is often recommended for removing grime.

Wearing protective gloves, I apply the polish with mutton cloth or a foam pad. I cover the outside surfaces and the immediately adjoining section of flue, which has a matching dark metal finish. I then use another cloth to rub all over and achieve a soft, graphite-like sheen. It will look like new.

Right: A quality woodburning stove is an investment, and if properly looked after it should last a lifetime. Cleaning it thoroughly once a year is a good habit to get into.

Your woodburner should be your pride and joy, so it is worth looking after it and keeping it in tip-top condition. It just needs attention every now and then as the need arises.

GLASS CLEANING

Trying to keep the glass on a woodburner's door clean can become something of an obsession. It looks better and more inviting if it is clean, and you get a far better idea of how the stove is functioning. The most obvious method is to use a scraper. These can be purpose-made, or you can buy a scraper that takes disposable knife blades, usually meant for cleaning paint off glass. After a while this gets harder to do, as the glass becomes more matt on the surface and chiselling off carbon can become a bit of a chore. Two things will help. One is doing it regularly so there isn't a heavy build-up in the first place, and the other is to use the stove correctly (see pages 88–90). Lastly, there are special woodburner cleaning fluids or compounds. Some may prefer not to resort to chemicals, but if it works, it works, and if the result is better than other methods, use it.

Above: Scrapers that are meant for cleaning paint off glass are ideal for keeping your woodburner's glass door clean.

ASH CLEARING

Ash is dusty and messy and will cling to the inside ledge of the woodburner's door and land on any ledges on the front of it as well as on the floor below. It is important to clear up any major mess promptly but it isn't necessary to sweep up every little outage of ash. We are quite house-proud, and a check on the dust level when the rooms are dusted once a week reveals there is a bit but not too much ash lying on shelves and other surfaces. If the stove were scrupulously dusted all the time, it would only cause more ash to fly around and land where it wasn't wanted. I use a hand vacuum in the mornings when the stove is cold and safe, and this removes ash efficiently and with ease.

TIP

The ash itself can be used as a glass cleaner, but wear a protective glove so you don't get in a mess. Just mix with a little water or vinegar, and rub.

Using our woodburner during weekday evenings and all day and evening at weekends results in my having to unload the ash pan just once at the start of the weekend. First I pick out any nails and so on from the grate while trying to keep the ash bed intact. Then I insert the ash-tray lifter into the fitting on the tray and put my thumb firmly over it so it cannot bounce loose and deposit a vast quantity of ash everywhere. Then I embark on a careful walk to the back door, avoiding humans, flapping curtains and pets before taking a steady walk down our back garden for final disposal. Doing this in a high wind is not advisable, for obvious reasons!

Above. Ash may seem like a messy, wasteful by-product, but it can benefit ornamental plants and vegetables greatly. It adds potash to the soil, which increases the pH level (that is, reduces acidity). However, this means it is unsuitable for plants that require acidic soil, such as rhododendrons, roses and fruit.

TIP

If you want to make use of ash in the garden, consult gardening books, online resources or your local horticultural society or garden centre to get the proper low-down on this quite complicated subject.

CLEARING UP DUST

If you do accidentally dump ash on the floor, the first thing to do is to stop children and pets from invading the space where it has happened. Remove any loose items, such as cushions and rugs, and, if necessary, place them in plastic refuse sacks to carry outdoors where they can be shaken and beaten to remove the ash dust. When you do so, it's advisable to use a simple dust mask to protect your lungs, and remember that ash will also stick to hair, skin and clothes.

Remove the bulk of any ash with a dustpan and brush, working slowly to avoid raising dust. The ash can then go straight into a plastic refuse sack which can be tied off and disposed of. You are then left with an insidious thin layer of dust on the floor, and possibly on the furniture. Although we think of ash as dirt, it is actually sterile and acts as a form of cleaning agent – it just doesn't look or feel good. The best procedure is to use an efficient vacuum cleaner with the appropriate cleaning head for hard floor, carpet or upholstery.

Lastly, all horizontal surfaces, on furniture, skirtings (baseboards) and ornaments, etc. need a light wipe with a damp cloth and maybe a polish to clean them and get rid of any dry grittiness. Once it is all sorted out, it won't be obvious that anything untoward has happened. After all, it's not like spilling a can of paint!

DISMANTLING AND REASSEMBLING YOUR WOOD STOVE

It's not a bad idea to go through this procedure once a year as winter approaches, just to make sure everything is in good order. Taking the innards of a woodburner apart varies according to the model.

TIP

Before taking the ash from the woodburner to wherever you intend to dispose of it, just make sure there are no trip hazards such as rucked carpet, toys or shoes lying around to catch you out. Assuming the ash pan is cold, it may be an idea to wrap it in a plastic rubbish sack so you avoid the risk of dumping ash on the floor completely.

With my woodburner, the grate front lifts out, then the baffle plate slides out from overhead in the firebox. The firebricks need to be pulled out sideways and carefully, since they get more fragile with use. Since my stove is a multifuel model, the centre section of the grate can then be popped out; as it does so, I have to carefully detach it from the rod that allows the grate to be riddled. Then the whole grate base itself lifts out, leaving the cast-iron casing as an empty shell.

The construction is pretty basic but it works, and while it is in this stripped-bare state I gently brush up the bulk of any remaining ash and then vacuum the rest. So long as nothing is cracked or broken, everything can be put back together. If any parts are damaged – which can happen occasionally because of heat cracking – then consult the parts list and contact your supplier or the manufacturer for a replacement. Your woodburner should not be operated without all of its essential components in place.

Above: Dismantling your stove can seem a daunting process. But, it shouldn't be, especially if you have the operating manual, which will show an exploded view of their parts. You can use a digital camera or smartphone to take photos of the various parts in position so it will help you to put everything back in the correct order.

TIP

While you are dismantling and checking your stove, don't forget to also check that the flue is intact and sealed properly to the stove, and that the register plate where the flue enters a chimney or exits a wall or ceiling is in position and sealed.

ORDERING SPARES

It pays to register your appliance when new, because this not only extends the warranty period but gives you full and easy access to the manufacturer's website, and you can then contact the makers if you need parts or advice. Alternatively, you can order spare parts through your local dealer. It may cost more, but they can give personal over-the-counter service. You will need to tell them the full part number as well as the name of the component, so you will need to refer to your manual.

Above: This is how firebricks look when they need replacing. Fitting new firebricks is easy enough, but their lightweight construction means that you need to take care not to break them as you install them.

FIREBRICK REPLACEMENT

Firebricks need replacement if they are cracked or badly pitted. Fitting new firebricks is not difficult, but you may find that the baffle plate, which sits above and between them, makes it harder to extract the bricks. In theory, pulling the baffle plate forward and off the cast lugs it sits on should get it out of the way, but you may not be able to remove it from the door opening because it jams. One trick is to remove the lower side bricks first so the top ones slide down, then remove those too, while keeping the baffle plate in place. Experience will show you what works best for the model that you have.

DOOR ROPE REPLACEMENT

The door rope does two things: it ensures that the rate of burn is controlled by the vents, not by door leaks; and it prevents unwanted and possibly dangerous fumes from polluting the atmosphere in the room. It will need replacing roughly every two or three years if the stove is well used. Change it when it gets frayed and fluffy.

Below: If your door rope looks frayed and fluffy like this, it is time to change it.

Use a flat-bladed screwdriver to dig into the cast slot where the rope sits in order to prise the rope out. Slide the screwdriver along the slot and the rope should come out fairly easily. Then work around the empty slot with the screwdriver to scrape any remaining traces of the old rope away.

To order a book, or to request a catalogue, contact: **GMC Publications Ltd**
Castle Place, 166 High Street, Lewes, East Sussex
BN7 1XU, United Kingdom
Tel: +44 (0)1273 488005
www.gmcbooks.com

The replacement needs to be the correct size; the parts diagram for the stove should show this. If you don't have that information you can check with your supplier, or pick one that looks right. So long as you keep the receipt and don't open the packaging, it can probably be returned for a refund if it's not the right kind.

The rope is usually round in section but the receiving slot may not be, and in any case when the door shuts, the rope gets flattened; therefore the correct rope size is one that may appear a bit large, but once compressed into place will be the correct shape and size to seal properly. A rope kit comes with a bottle of adhesive and the fitting procedure is as follows:

Hold the rope in position all around the door-seal slot. Check the length, then wrap a piece of adhesive tape around the rope at that point and cut it with scissors – slightly overlength, so there is no danger of a gap when installed. Apply the adhesive to the bottom of the slot all the way round and then position the rope; I would suggest with the join at the hinge side of the door. Now push the rope into the slot firmly, working all the way round until the ends meet tightly together.

You now need to start a slow-burning fire, or at least one that will burn itself out after a while. The purpose of this is to warm the adhesive so it dries, but not make it so hot that it fails to adhere properly. Close the door, open again to make sure the rope is still in the slot, close the door and then let the fire burn out, with the vents partially closed so the stove doesn't get too hot. Your woodburner is now fully prepared for use, and next time you light it the rope will do its job.

TIP

Check your stove regularly, just like you would a car, to ensure it is safe. When the stove is cold it is easy to look around inside and out, just to be sure everything is in good working order. And don't forget to test your carbon monoxide detector, too.

SWEEPING THE CHIMNEY

However careful you are with your burn settings, it is inevitable that there will be a build-up of deposits in the flue. To avoid the risk of a chimney fire, it is recommended that a chimney be swept twice a year if you're burning wood, and once a year if you're burning smokeless fuel.

A woodburner should be connected to a flue, not an open chimney. Where an existing chimney is used with a flue lining, the lining is a concertina type that is dropped down from the chimney pot on the roof above and is capable of bypassing obstacles, such as where an upstairs fireplace interferes with the flow of the chimney shape. Smoothing out the flue shape in this way makes it easier to sweep properly, as well as sealing the exhaust gases and smoke into the flue until they leave the chimney pot at the top. Where a separate flue using rigid pipes has been installed instead, sweeping should be no problem; there may be access hatches if the flue pipe is cranked in shape.

TIP

Wear suitable clothes so it doesn't matter if they get dirty, and drape an old curtain over the entire stove area so only the chimney-sweep rods can get underneath. This will ensure that any deposits that spill out are contained on the hearth.

It is recommended that a chimney be swept twice a year if you're burning wood, and once a year if you're burning smokeless fuel.

It is possible to buy a set of rods and a brush and sweep the chimney yourself. It isn't difficult, as I have found out. It needs to be done in time for winter, so you know the flue is clear of tarry deposits and other obstructions. It isn't as messy as cleaning an open chimney – that is strictly a job for a professional, not just because of the mess but also the need to clean the irregular shape properly and remove soot. Soot is not an issue with a woodburner, as tar is the only deposit.

SWEEPING AWAY THE TAR DEPOSITS
INSIDE THE CHIMNEY LINER

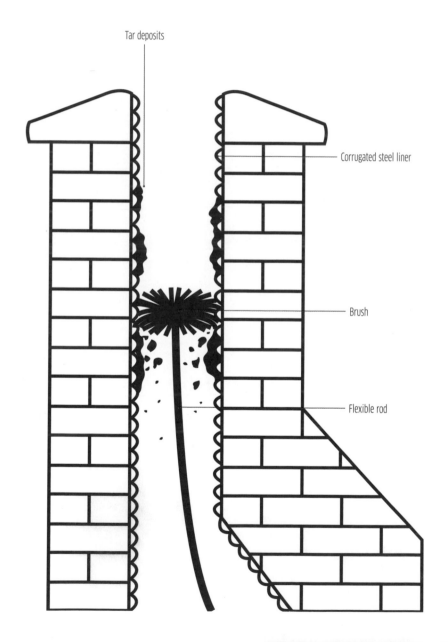

Tar deposits

Corrugated steel liner

Brush

Flexible rod

You will be on hands and knees and should wear old clothes, although it isn't such a messy business as you might imagine. The first job is to remove the baffle plate to gain access to the flue. The baffle plate will shed a lot of fallen flue deposits as you lift it out. The next thing is to push the brush head firmly into the base of the flue and ram the rods in, bearing in mind that they will be bending in a tight curve in order to negotiate the firebox and move up into the flue. Once the first sections disappear from view, screw on more rods and continue. A forwards and backwards action will dislodge deposits as you go. They will clatter down the flue and into the hearth area, which needs to be clear of anything not connected with sweeping.

Above: If this is the first time you've swept a chimney, don't forget to take a photo of the brush poking out at the top, just for the record!

A forwards and backwards action will dislodge tar deposits as you go. They will clatter down the flue and into the hearth area.

Eventually, the brush should exit the chimney pot and come free (or emerge into the cowl if there is one), as it is no longer squashed in the flue. Go outside and check that it is so. Then pull the brush and attached rods back down; this will remove further deposits, and hopefully by the time it is out of the stove all the loose matter will have been removed and will be lying in the stove and on the hearth. Unthread the rods one by one and draw the brush out of the stove. Finally, get a dustpan and brush to clear up, and finish off with vacuum cleaner.

TIP

Should you prefer to have the job done professionally for peace of mind and to avoid mess, there are chimney sweeps in all areas who can perform this service. They should provide a certificate to show the work has been done to a good standard, and they will bring dust sheets and a vacuum. Their training and experience will minimize mess and disruption.

Glossary

Baffle plate An insert in the upper part of a stove which deflects the hot gases into an S-shaped path.

Bow saw A compact frame saw used for lopping branches or cutting narrow-diameter tree trunks.

Cap or cowl A ventilated cover placed on the top of a chimney. Although not essential, it will protect against ingress of rain and prevent birds nesting on the chimney.

Catalyst Some stoves have a catalyst rather like a car exhaust catalyst. It scrubs the chimney smoke, making a stove more suitable for smokeless zones.

Chainsaw A petrol or electric power machine with a chain cutter that has teeth all along it. Used to cut large branches and tree trunks. Proper training, licensing and safety wear are essential.

Coppicing An ancient technique of harvesting relatively young timber. It tends to be used for wattle fencing and such like; it is less effective as a firewood because the sections of branch are quite small. The trees have the branches removed above ground level, allowing new branches to shoot from around the base to cropped in the future.

Cordwood Wood that has been cut and tied together in bundles for burning.

Door rope An essential non-asbestos plaited rope designed to withstand great heat and held in place with a special adhesive compound.

Dry wood Any timber, whether dead, felled, air-dried or kiln-dried, that contains only a limited amount of water in the form of sap within the cells of the wood.

Firebricks Insulating bricks that hold the heat of a fire in so that the heat is directed where the bricks are not and to protect the casing of a woodburner from excessive heat, which could damage it.

Flue A solid pipe that conveys smoke from a stove into the chimney above, or directly to the outside of the building.

Flue liner Where a stove flue feeds into a chimney, a flue liner runs inside the flue up the chimney to the roof where it meets the chimney pot.

Froe A tool for splitting wood, consisting of a narrow blade attached at right angles to a handle. By striking the back of the blade and by twisting it, the log can be split throughout its length.

Grate There are two basic types: one is designed for wood fuel and cannot be riddled, i.e. moved to shake ash; the second can be moved vigorously in a multifuel stove to loosen and drop clinker into the ash pan underneath.

Hand axe Although meant for lopping, a standard hand axe can be used for further splitting of smaller split logs.

Hearth A solid fireproof surface on which an open fire or a woodburner can be safely operated.

Kindling Fine split wood or light branches which are used to start a fire as the flame and oxygen can reach all the surfaces easily and help combustion speed up or take place.

Multifuel stove A stove type that will accept any fuel within its designed capacity, e.g. logs, smokeless fuel and briquettes.

Primary airflow The air flowing through the lower vents in a stove. When burning wood rather than smokeless fuels, a bed of ash normally obstructs the airflow.

Primary burn The burning of fuel within the grate of the stove.

Pruning saw A saw for pruning branches. Modern versions have lethal 'shark-teeth' blades and a pistol-grip handle. They are very versatile when cleaning up branches and trunks.

Register plate A metal plate that seals off the bottom of a chimney in a fireplace, and contains an opening for the flue to pass through it. It ensures a safe, sealed system and prevents soot and dust falling into the room.

Secondary airflow Air taken into the stove from the ambient air in the room. Some installations have an additional external air supply duct to help the fire without taking too much air from the room.

Secondary burn The further combustion of gases from the fire as they move upwards around the baffle plate and into the flue.

Sledgehammer A large construction hammer made of steel with a wooden or composite handle. It comes in several sizes; if you plan to use it with splitting wedges, choose a hammer that is heavier than the wedges.

Smokeless zone (smoke control area) In some towns and cities in the UK, USA and many other countries, this is a legally enforceable zone designed to protect the urban atmosphere from excessive pollution.

Splitting axe This has a wider head than a standard tree axe designed for felling or lopping, so it can withstand the forces of parting logs ready for burning.

Splitting maul A long-handled tool with a short, blunt head, usually with one axe-like face and an alternative flat face for hitting splitting wedges. It may incorporate a hook to help separate a partly split log.

Splitting wedge A long, heavy, steel wedge, designed to part awkward logs along the grain. Hit with a maul or sledgehammer, it is best used as one of a pair, to ensure a full split and effective retrieval of the first wedge if it gets trapped.

Tarring A hardened residue in the flue liner, as a result of incomplete combustion. It can be minimized by setting the vents correctly and by regular chimney sweeping.

Venturi effect A reduction in the pressure of air (or any other fluid) when it flows through a constricted space.

Water box Fitted to the back of a stove, a water box supplies hot water to a connected radiator system.

Wet wood Wood that is 'green', i.e. freshly cut and containing a lot of wet tree sap.

Useful websites

UK

Forestry Commission
A valuable source of information relating to forestry, grants, wood fuel sources and environmental matters.
www.forestry.gov.uk

National Biofuel Database
Find your local suppliers of wood fuel, filtered by accreditation and fuel type.
www.woodfueldirectory.org

Woodsure
A wood fuel quality assurance scheme for finding reputable suppliers.
www.woodsure.co.uk

HETAS
The government-recognized official body for solid-fuel and biomass heating regulation relating to appliances, fuels, installers and servicing.
www.hetas.co.uk

Small Woodlands Owners Group
Find out about events, woodland wildlife and ancient forests, and share knowledge about woodland ownership.
www.swog.org.uk

Woodlands.co.uk
A business with environmental stewardship as a key aspect, selling small parcels of woodland.
www.woodlands.co.uk

USA

US Forest Service
A section of the Department of Agriculture which has a brief covering all aspects of forestry.
www.fs.fed.us

US Environmental Agency
Responsible for all aspects of environmental protection. The website has valuable advice about woodburners as well as information about legislation and enforcement with regard to woodburning.
www.epa.gov

Land Watch
A website for locating all kinds of land for sale, including woodland.
www.landwatch.com

About the **author**

ANTHONY BAILEY has had a varied career that splits roughly into thirds during his working life. The first third was as a photographic assistant and then a studio photographer in London; the next third was as an antique furniture restorer, furniture designer/maker and maker of bespoke kitchens and joinery; and the current third is as a woodworking journalist and editor. Having been technical editor and editor on several woodworking magazines including *Woodworking Plans & Projects*, and the launch editor of *Woodworking Crafts*, he has also found time to write books such as *Routing for Beginners*, *Router Jigs and Templates* and *Success With Biscuit Joiners*.

PICTURE CREDITS

Anthony Bailey: 47 (bottom), 48, 57 (right), 70, 71, 91 (top), 91 (bottom), 93, 96, 99, 100 (top), 100 (bottom), 101, 104, 109; *Charnwood*: cover image, 4, 6, 9, 16, 31, 37, 82, 112; *Jonathan Bailey*: 95; *Jotul*: 26, 30; *Morso*: 21, 85 (top left, top right, centre left, centre right, bottom left), 88; *Photocase*: Triveo (10), vagner (12), birdys (59) *rebelxned/Flickr*: 76–77; *Shutterstock*: unpict (1), Ververidis Vasilis (8), melis (10–11), Kryvenok Anastasiia (13, top), berna namoglu (13, bottom), viki2win (14–15), the goatman (29), Alexander Tihonov (32–33), Hanna Alandi (34), cdrin (35), Virunja (40), fotofred (42), Mikhail Olykainen (45), petr73 (46), Jo millington (47, top), Olesya Kuznetsova (50–51), carlos castilla (52), David Maixner (58), Anki Hoglund (61), Praewachimi (62), hraska (63), LianeM (64), Ruud Morijn Photographer (65), Jon Bilous (67), Noerenberg (73), Robsonphoto (79), Peter Guess (80–81), unpict (86), VSem (87), ARENA Creative (89), alexkich (90), mady70 (94), Ami Parikh (97); *Thinkstock*: iStock/ bartosz_zakrzewski (15), iStock/PetanelaART (49), iStock/leekris (54), Hemera/Nedim Juki (56–57), iStock/Trevor Buchanan (81, right).

Index